Lesotho

BY DIRK AND COLLEEN SCHWAGER

Published by Dirk Schwager
             Photographic Illustrations
             Cape Town

© Dirk and Colleen Schwager 1972

ISBN 0-620-00688-9

—

Printed in the Republic of South Africa by

Edson-Clyde Press (Pty) Ltd, Cape Town

Lithographic Positives by Hirt and Carter (Pty) Ltd

Bound by Edward D. Seabrook, Cape Town

Set in 12pt Perpetua

Cover design by Tony Butler

CONTENTS

INTRODUCTION

The scent of things has the power to recall, for a moment, but so vividly, whole chunks of experience. And these recollections are probably a lot more real, a lot nearer the truth, than pages of relevant facts, theories and statistics. To see and smell the smoke from the warm brown huts, seeping through their thatch, clinging in coils and tatters to the mountain sides, slipping into the valleys, is so much more real, so much more permanent, than speculation as to the effectiveness of colonial rule in the late 19th century. Dawn in Lesotho has a translucence and stillness which can only be conveyed by being there, at that time, in the mountains. The unforgettable scent of cow dung fires and the soft greyness of their smoke, is as much Lesotho as the small hard hooves of Basuto ponies, stepping deftly between the rocks, as the bizarre colours and patterns of blankets, as the early morning sunlight that gives each goat a silvery aura of light.

Another scent is the astringent fragrance of wild mint. This grows in masses of tough, grey green bushes, clumped in gulleys and along the streams. The streams are bubbly and clear, rushing over round brown stones, and so very drinkable. As you lie on your stomach, drinking the clean, cold water, the heat of the sun draws out the scent of mint so intensely that you drink it with the water. The hot middays and the smell of mint; herdboys, everywhere the herdboys, laughing, shy, splashing in the falling water; their dogs, quiet and watching. The Basuto are so fond of this herb that they stuff thick wads of it into their nostrils. One can see them, walking with a loose, rhythmic gait, along the miles of winding paths, up and down the valleys with tufts of grey green leaves protruding from their noses, consciously savouring the wild mint of Lesotho.

The expression 'living silence' is often used in descriptions of Africa. There are so many kinds of living silence. In the Malutis, the silence is pure and bracing like the air. At that altitude, sound carries, echoing and rebounding between the mountains, as, without drums, the Basuto pass along messages; clear ringing calls, from mountaintop to mountaintop. Silence is also a visible thing. Few sights are more descriptive of silence than silhouettes. As poignant as the scents and silence in Lesotho, are the silhouettes. The immense emptiness and colour of the evening skies behind the outline of a man on his horse, blanket pinned at the shoulder, conical grass hat, an echo of the hut, motionless, before descending into the valleys again. Everything casts a long shadow and silhouette. Outlines are hard and clear because the air is clean and dry. The rigid aloes, all symmetrical arms, the huts, the donkeys, adorn the sky-line, which divides everything in half, solid black earth, great clear skies.

French painters in the nineteenth century were searching for 'white' light. They would have found it in Lesotho. So stainless is the air, that after summer storms, the rays of light, refracted by the momentary vapour, form brilliant rainbows, reflecting in softer shadows of the shadow of the rainbow. Colours are muted by distance only. Blue mountains become unbelievably purple. Even the red-gold expanses of thatching grass become purple when reaching the mountains. The winter landscapes are compositions of the most stirring colours. Stark red ploughed fields, white dry grass, ten shades of purple, charcoal and gold. And then the snow. In dryness and dust and red earth, snow, dry powdery snow, frozen streams, icicles in the tufts of red grass by the pools, icy white encroaching upon the brown and purple.

We've spoken of the silence in Lesotho. An inhabited silence, because in Lesotho there is no absolute solitude. One can ride for days through the remotest areas of the country without encountering a single living soul, but stop to rest and you become aware of being watched; soon you will be joined by someone, usually a herdboy. These boys speak very little but smile easily. Sent out with the cattle from the age of six these children spend months away from the village, living from the land and a bag of mieliemeal, sheltering in the stone huts built for them at special vantage points. They keep the cattle out in the mountains for the period between late summer and late winter. When grazing begins to fail and the temperatures drop too low, they return home for the cattle to feed on the remains of the crops just reaped. These herdboys embody something of the soul of Lesotho, because they are one of the timeless features of the country. A hundred years ago, with the same smiles, bearing the same responsibilities, sent out with nothing beside a pot and a bag of meal, these boys herded the wealth of their villages.

The centres of activity in the mountains are the missions and the trading stores, usually close together. The network of bridlepaths connects the villages with these centres. More often than not, the only access to these settlements is by means of the bridlepaths and a landing strip, visited a few times a week by a single engined plane. The children's modelled clay toys demonstrate the development from ponies and donkeys to Lockheeds and Cessnas! The glorious absence of scrapheaps, of twisted metal of any kind, is a singular blessing in our polluted world. A more tangible blessing is the musicality of the Basutos. Go into the church on one of these mission stations and listen to the spontaneous instinctive four part harmony of the singing. His Grace, the Very Reverend Archbishop Mabathoane, first Basuto Archbishop, has captured all the harmony and religious emotion of his people in his setting for the Mass in Sesuto. This is always sung at Midnight Mass on Christmas Eve at the Cathedral in Maseru. It is an experience no-one should forego.

Because the geography of the country makes road-building an almost out-of-the-question proposition except in the foothills and in the most pressing of cases, one rides or flies in Lesotho. Flying undeniably gives a tremendous overall impression of the country, but it can never usurp the horse. This encounter with Lesotho, days of trekking through the mountains on a Basuto pony, is a great adventure. It brings the correct perspective into one's experience. These ponies are capable of carrying one an average of 60 to 70 kilometres a day, involving ascents and descents of over a thousand metres 3 or 4 times in that distance, and the going is incredibly hard, despite paths. Few horses in the world are capable of these feats. Ever since Moshesh, founder and chief of the Basuto, first sat on a horse, very quickly mastering the art of riding it, the horse has become native to Lesotho. During the South African War, both Boer and British troops were paying £50 apiece for Basuto ponies.

The smell of horses is another integral part of Lesotho: the pungent, moist smell of a sweating pony, mingling with dust. The winters are dry, and with dryness comes the all penetrating fragrant dust; the clean dust of fine blown earth.

Lesotho

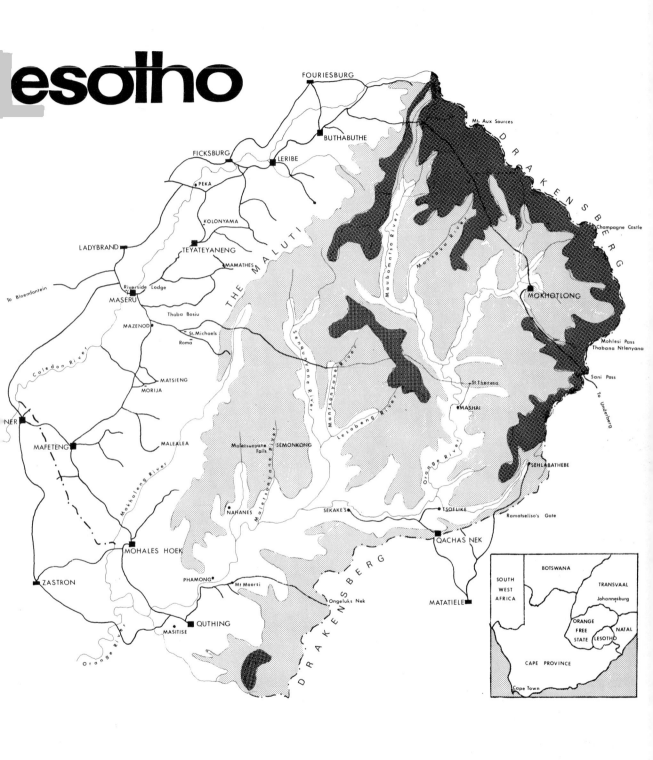

FOURIESBURG

Mt. Aux Sources

D R A K E N S B E R G

BUTHABUTHE

FICKSBURG

LERIBE

PEKA

Champagne Castle

KOLONYAMA

LADYBRAND

TEYATEYANENG

MAMATHES

THE MALUTI

Maubamio River

Martatukju River

To Bloemfontein

Riverside Lodge

MASERU

Thaba Bosiu

Senqunyane River

MAZENOD

St. Michaels

Roma

MOKHOTLONG

Mohlesi Pass
Thabana Ntlenyana

MATSIENG

MORIJA

Mantonyane River

Letobeng River

Sani Pass

To Underberg

St. Theresa

MASHAI

NER

MAFETENG

MALEALEA

Maletsuayane Falls

SEMONKONG

Malelibyane River

Makhaleng River

SEHLABATHEBE

Orange River

NAHANES

SEKAKE'S

TSOELIKE

Ramatseliso's Gate

MOHALES HOEK

QACHAS NEK

ZASTRON

PHAMONG

Mt Moorsi

D R A K E N S B E R G

Ongeluks Nek

MATATIELE

QUTHING

MASITISE

Orange River

BOTSWANA

SOUTH
WEST
AFRICA

TRANSVAAL

Johannesburg

ORANGE
FREE
STATE

NATAL

LESOTHO

CAPE PROVINCE

Cape Town

GEOGRAPHY

Fifty million years before the Alpine ranges of Europe and Asia were heaved into existence, the Malutis of Lesotho were being sculptured into their present form by the elements. The study of geological periods is a subduing experience and in Lesotho it is the antiquity of the landscape as much as its immensity which dwarfs one.

Lesotho is eccentrically situated within the Republic of South Africa. It is bounded on the West by the Orange Free State, on the east by Natal and East Griqualand and in the South by the Cape Province. Topographically the country is governed by the drainage areas of the two principal rivers, the Orange and the Caledon (known in Lesotho as the Mokhare and the Senqua rivers). It is a fascinating concept that what starts as an ooze in the boggy wastes of the high plateaux of the Malutis, is finally a turgid torrent hurling thousands of tons of soil into the Atlantic at Luderitz. Two thirds of Lesotho is almost impenetrable mountain. Somewhere in the middle the Malutis become the Drakensberge, gathering themselves into the peaks of Thaba Ntlenyame, the highest point in Southern Africa and Mont aux Sources. The principal tributaries of the Orange are the Malibamatso and the Senqunyane. Another is the Malutsanyane, and the gorges of these rivers sink deep into the Sandstone rock and volcanic basalt of the mountains. The Malutsanyane gorge is headed by the highest straight drop waterfall in Africa. For two hundred metres the waters of the Malutsanyane hurtle silently through space into this stupendous canyon. I saw these falls first at sunset. The bottom of the gorge was already in darkness and too far away for the roar of the water to be heard. The last rays of the sun struck obliquely into the gorge illuminating a perfect rainbow, arching from the bottom to the top of the falls. As striking as the vastness of the spectacle was its immense silence.

Ninety-nine percent of the rocks of Lesotho range from the Triassic to the Lower Jurassic ages. Throughout the world these strata are characterised by a peculiar reptilian fauna. The super-order of dinosaurs made their appearance in middle Triassic times. So we may very well picture the lowlands of Lesotho as having been the primeval playground of romping dinosaurs! There are nine kinds of fossilised dinosaur footprints at Leribe.

Most of the soils of Lesotho are Stormberg in origin. In the mountains the soils are basaltic in origin or derive from the Cave Sandstone rock which lies beneath the volcanic basalt. The rock strata are generally parallel with the surface and the soils, where not eroded, are often deep and fertile. The Volcanic eruptions which give the country its characteristic basalt formations also bequeathed Lesotho pipes of Kimberlite and with this, considerable diamond deposits. Not only does the Orange River carry topsoil to the ocean, the alluvial diamond fields of South West Africa are scattered with gems washed from the 'blue ground' in Lesotho.

Mountain country is by nature very susceptible to natural erosion. Due to excessive cultivation and overgrazing, gully erosion (donga formation) is common in the loose soils of the lowlands. On the hilltops there is also considerable 'sliding' erosion, where large portions of soil, bound by roots of plants and grasses, slide down over the smooth surfaces of underlying sandstone often only ten centimetres below the soil. Wind erosion of cultivated land is common and a heavy downpour of rain may remove large sheets of soil from planted lands. Extensive anti-erosion measures are being carried out in the country and the recovery of much indigenous flora is rapid.

The average rainfall for Lesotho varies from about 650 millimetres in the southern mountains to about 750 millimetres in the North. It is not rare though, for the rainfall in the Oxbow region of the north to be as high as 2000 millimetres. Much of this rain comes in the form of violent thunderstorms and is so heavy that most of the water runs rapidly into numerous small streams and rivers which feed the larger rivers. Steady soaking rain, known as 'Molupe' is common later in the summer however, and traditionally lasts three days. The benefits are startlingly apparent in the incredible growth of grass and crops afterwards.

Snow may fall in Lesotho in the mountains at any time of the year, and in winter the mountain regions experience snow for weeks on end. In the lowlands snowfalls are possible between March and September. A particularly lovely phenomenon is the occasional spring snowstorm when the peach trees are a mass of pink blossom. In general the temperatures are consistent, with a summer maximum of 90°F and winter minimum of −8°F. It may freeze at any time in the mountains where altitudes above 2400 metres are often subject to freak storms.

The wonderful open landscape of Lesotho, with razor sharp horizons, is due to its being principally a grassland. There is comparatively little natural bush or tree growth. In the lowlands the most common and the most exciting silhouette is that of the introduced American Aloe (Agave Americana). These are planted to make 'living' kraals, and in spring thrust out flowering stems of three to six metres high. The flowers are often cut to feed cattle. These aloes dry in winter and provide lightweight yet strong building poles. A good strong fibre similar to Sisal can be obtained from the leaves and a certain amount of fuel from the dead plants. In the absence of fir-trees the Europeans in Lesotho have taken to decorating these bizarre plants as Christmas trees. The dried seed-pods seem to have been developed solely to hold the Christmas candles!

One plant entirely confined to the mountains of Lesotho and therefore very rare is the Spiral Aloe (Aloe Polyphylla). Even in Lesotho this species has a limited distribution. Among the several species of grasses on the mountain slopes are a number of varieties of Erica, which sometimes cover whole hillsides. The highest regions of the country are wide, shallow, boggy valleys providing a close compact sward, usually heavily grazed and closely covered with low growing flowers. The tall red-hot-poker with its blue green leaves (Kniphofia Caulescens) often covers acres of ground in damp places. And at Easter the weed, Cosmos, with its myriad flowers of pink, magenta and white, covers loose sandbanks, neglected grain fields and winds in ribbons of colour on the grass banks between the fields.

In summer Lesotho is green, it begins to fade in autumn. It becomes straw-coloured, except for the red gold thatching grass (Hyparrwenia Ssp) which is carefully preserved in certain valleys and hillslopes.

HISTORY

'KE BONA LESELI! I have seen the light. As down broke each day, Moshesh, founder of the Basotho nation, would emerge from his hut with this greeting. Tradition has it that he adopted this habit during the terrible Difaqane wars which seared the interior of Southern Africa in the years between 1820 and 1830, when the probability of being murdered in the night by marauding tribes was so great that the dawning of each new day wrang this spontaneous cry from Moshesh. The small, scattered Sotho-speaking clans were almost totally destroyed by this outbreak of savage killing. Moshesh, young chief of his clan, then living near Butha Buthe, desperate to preserve his tribe, trekked to Thaba Basiu. Here on this superb natural fortress, the infant nation was able to defend itself against incredible odds and survived. Moshesh's symbolic cry had prophetic significance. Few leaders of men have been more enlightened and so far in advance of their time as this warrior of the small Bamokoteli tribe. The Basuto owe their existence to this truly remarkable combination of gentleness, sensitivity and wisdom in one man, Moshesh.

The emergence of the Basuto nation coincided with troubled times in central Southern Africa. In all probability it was this very adversity coupled with the leadership of Moshesh that created a situation out of which the Basuto came into existence as an individual nation.

Moshesh's youth, as heir to the chieftainship of the Bamokoteli clan, was idyllic. (The Bamokoteli were an offshoot of the Bakuena.) Sotho-speaking clans were scattered all over the territory west of the Drakensberge, south of the Limpopo and north of the Orange. They kept fairly substantial cattle herds and also planted sorghum, each clan living relatively independently of the other. At odd times one chief would become more influential than his neighbours, who would secure his neutrality if not protection by paying him certain tithes. Sporadic cattle-thieving would result in spasmodic retaliatory raids, but in general, tribal life was uncomplicated by any larger hierarchical structure or over ambitious chiefs. Many clans enjoyed extremely cordial relations and there was a fair amount of inter-marriage.

It was in this setting that the first whisper of impending disaster was heard. The chief of the Bamonaheng clan, Mohlomi, was a wise, peace-loving old man and also a renowned seer and rain-maker. This man had such perception and insight into the spirit-world that he was visited by devotees from all over the interior. To-day, the newly established hospital for psychiatric disease outside Maseru pays tribute to Mohlomi by bearing his name. Moshesh in particular, entertained a great love for Mohlomi whose teachings which were the greatest single influence on the young man. It was on the advice of Mohlami for example that Moshesh became a total abstainer, a habit he rigidly adhered to all his life. Many years later, in conversations with the French missionary, Eugene Casalis, Moshesh related that upon inquiring what potions he should take in order to gain wisdom and power, Mohlomi replied that these gifts were not dependent on medicine but on clarity of mind, goodness of heart and service to one's fellow man. (*Becker op. cit. p. 18 *Hill of Destiny*).

On his deathbed, Mohlomi spoke of red dust clouds rising in the east, bringing with them mighty warfaring tribes which would decimate the defenceless Sotho tribes and usher in an age of famine, slaughter, cannibalism and fratricide. At this time the Sotho tribes in the interior were ignorant of the vast war-machine being set in motion by Shaka, the Zulu, east of the Drakensberge. Reverberations of pillage and slaughter were soon to shake these small tribes to their foundations. A series of severe droughts in quick succession brought poverty and revolt among the tribes. Fugitives from Shaka's reign of terror had formed raiding bands, and by 1821 the scene was set for the Difaqane tragedy.

Moshesh, now popularly acclaimed chief of the clan, had established his own kraal near what is now known as Butha Buthe. The rising tide of the Difaqane forced him to flee, with a pitifully small band of the Bamokoteli to the flat-topped mountain in the south, later to be called Thaba Bosiu (Mountain of the Night). On this perilous trek, his grandfather, Peete, bringing up the rear, was captured and eaten by cannibals before he could be rescued. Settled with his tribe on Thaba Bosiu, Moshes grew to full maturity as leader of the infant Basuto nation. The Difaqane was slowly burning itself out, leaving in its wake the ghastly spectacle of famine-crazed bands of tribesmen having resorted to cannibalism for survival. These bands of savages, completely demented by their own depravity, withdrew into caves, in the mountains where they lived under sub-human conditions. Moshesh maintained that the cannibals could be rehabilitated by readmittance to village life, kindness and understanding. His councillors clamoured for their execution. This attitude of Moshesh's to the cannibal problem was a clear demonstration of an insight and understanding of human relationships which, though assuring immortality of his name, gradually started a process of alienation from his own tribesmen. This is a tragic phenomenon. A man of ability and compassion, slowly, despite all his efforts, losing touch with his rapidly growing Basuto nation.

On Thaba Bosiu and its immediate vicinity he continued to rule, loved and revered by all around him. There is ample record of this by Eugene Casalis, the first missionary to Lesotho, at Moshesh's own insistence, and one of the very first white men ever encountered by the Basuto. A very interesting and warm relationship developed between the young Frenchman and the middleaged chief. Eugene Casalis had been sent to South Africa by the Paris Evangelical Missionary Society, and arrived at Thaba Bosiu on the 28th June 1833. This day was regarded by Moshesh as one of the most important days in the history of the Basuto people.

Moshesh gave the missionaries, Casalis, Arbouset, and Gosselin, Morija as the site for their mission. Later Casalis moved to the foot of Thaba Bosiu and built a church and house there, in order to be close to his friend, Moshesh.

In contrast to his contemporaries, Mzilikazi, chief of the Matabele, Sikonyela, chief of the Wild Cat People, Shaka, and Dingane, respectively chiefs of the Zulus who ruled by terror, Moshesh cultivated among his people confidence and love. It is recorded by the missionaries that in their prayers they never ceased to thank God for the privilege of living and working in the domain of so wise and loving a ruler.

It was, however, this very kindliness which slowly lost him the obedience of the more far-flung Basuto kraals. More and more fugitives had come to Thaba Bosiu to seek protection. These people were always warmly welcomed by Moshesh and given gifts of cattle and grain and a place to build their huts. By 1850 the Basuto numbered over 70 000. Events in the Cape Colony and the movement of the Boers away from British Rule had resulted in the settlement of many Boer families in the area between the Vaal and Orange Rivers.

Moshesh's problem with his new neighbours was basically a conflict between two entirely different systems of land ownership and use. A boundary was a concept unknown to Africans. Wherever there were Basuto owing allegiance to Moshesh, the land they grazed and tilled was his responsibility; and in this sense it could be said that his domain extended far into the territory now known as the Orange Free State. Cattle raids by the Basuto, apart from the theft angle were, to the Boers, intrusion inside their boundaries. Any support by Moshesh of these people was then considered active support of the mischief makers and not merely a natural defence of Basuto grazing rights.

Had the situation included only Boer and Basuto, Moshesh with his fine sense of diplomacy and skill in negotiation would undoubtedly have reached and understanding with the Boers; possibly by submitting to restrictions of the land under his sway. There was, however, the presence of the British. It was here that Eugene Casalis, who had a diplomatic sense as fine as Moshesh's and a far wider knowledge of the world, stepped into the position of the chief's political adviser, in effect, foreign secretary. It was on Casalis' advice that Moshesh developed a friendship with the British that became the core of his policy.

Complicating things further were developments within the Basuto nation. Where borders are arbitrary, clashes are inevitable. Moshesh's sons and younger chieftains became impatient with his conciliatory policies and began taking the law into their own hands. Moshesh's constant refusal to deal harshly with miscreants resulted in a general loosening of control. There was misinterpretation of this foreign situation by British officials to the British Government. This was a time too, when men shot at sight, when for the Boers, even more than for the

Basuto, who had their mountains to retreat to, the issue was human existence. In this build-up of tensions between Boer settlers, British Administration and the Sotho tribes, Moshesh repeatedly emerged as a natural diplomat, behaving with dignity and integrity in the most complex and dangerous situations.

Nevertheless, circumstances made war inevitable. This was a tragic development as Moshesh had achieved, at a personal level, warm and sincere relationships with both Boer and British leaders of the time. In 1858 the Free State declared war on the Basuto. This war lasted a month and was an indeterminate affair. Mediation by Sir George Grey, Governor of the Cape, left both sides exasperated. Moshesh, taking stock of the situation, saw that his only hope of continued security would be to bring Basutoland under the direct suzerainty of Queen Victoria. From this time on he worked toward this objective. However, astute ruler that he was, he wanted British protection but not British law and British magistrates. This, he said, "would be a stone too heavy for my people to carry". The British were aware of this and negotiations dragged on for the next ten years.

Eugene Casalis was recalled to France by his Church in March 1855. This was a tremendous blow to Moshesh, and the beginning of a steady process of increasing alienation from all about him. His first and chief wife, Mamahato, the mother of his four chief sons, Letsie, Molapo, Masupha and Majara, had died some years before. It is reliably recorded that he had been extremely attached to Mamahato and felt her loss deeply. His sons were no comfort to him and the companionship of two sons from other wives was also denied him when one died and the other left to establish his own kraal in East Griqualand.

The constant tension and bitterness which was mounting yearly all about him began to tell. By 1862 Moshesh was a tired and disillusioned man. The great drought of 1862 caused fresh outbreaks of thieving by clans threatened with starvation. Moshesh, now ill, became obstinate, refusing to recognise the boundaries proposed by the Boers. He nevertheless continued to do his utmost to avert the horror of war despite violent opposition from his hot-headed tribesmen. It was only when he appealed to them with tears streaming down his lined cheeks that his dignitaries agreed to bear with him once more. Moshesh's gesture in moving settled Basuto families from the Winberg and Harrismith districts was brought to naught by a general outbreak of raids all along the borders. On the 9th June 1865, President Brand declared war, and the major invasion of Lesotho took place in mid-July 1865. Moshesh, it was reported, took to his bed ill, tired and lonely.

The prolonged and desultory campaigns between Boer and Basuto were brought to a stop by the annexation of Basutoland by Sir Phillip Woodehouse on behalf of Her Majesty Queen Victoria and the British Government on March 12th 1868.

Moshesh was now failing fast and his last two years were lonely and bitter, brightened only by visits of Adele Mabille, daughter of Eugene Casalis. Moshesh had loved his "Delly" ever since she'd been born at the French Mission at the foot of Thaba Bosiu. To her he said ". . . do not forsake me, and do not weary of praying for me, perhaps God will answer your prayers."

In 1870, shortly before his death, he told Adele Mabille that he was at peace at last, and agreed to be baptised on the 12th March. All were invited to Thaba Bosiu for the event and elaborate preparations were made. On the morning of March 11th, however, his spirits came to fetch him. A mound of stones was piled over his grave on Thaba Bosiu and a simple slab of stone bore a solitary name – Moshesh.

Although his conflict with the Boers had greatly reduced his power, he had succeeded in what he set out to do. He had gathered the oppressed and wandering Sotho people about him, given them horses and weapons for their protection and moulded them into a nation. He had brought them the means of learning and enlightenment and shown them the path of security and peace. He had introduced and encouraged a doctrine which, though he himself never formally accepted, had the key to a better age. He had secured them British protection needed to guide them in times increasingly difficult to understand. Moshesh, in the history of the Basuto stands as the link between primitive and modern Africa.

Initially Basutoland came under the administration of the Cape Colony. This did not prove very successful. Cape politicians being resentful of this additional burden and the Basuto none too confident that the Cape Government would aid them against their Boer neighbours with whom relations were still strained.

The discovery of diamonds in 1870 at what was later to be known as Kimberley, ushered in a new period of development for Basutoland. The diamond rush, and so too the Gold rush on the Witwatersrand in 1886, brought urgent demands for labour, wheat, slaughter and transport cattle. It became a period of comparative prosperity for Basutoland. Much of the new wealth was invested in firearms. In 1878 the Cape Parliament passed a Peace Preservation Act, making it illegal for Africans to purchase or possess arms. Naturally this was bitterly resented and culminated in the Gun War of 1880-81, in which the Basuto, under the leadership of the Paramount Chief Letsie's son, Lerotholi, a worthy descendant of his grandfather, Moshesh, were successful in forcing the Cape authorities to come to terms. Negotiations with Britain were brought under way and on the 18th March 1884, Basutoland became a Crown Colony and the administration was placed in the hands of a Resident Commissioner, Sir Marshall Clarke, responsible to the Governor of the Cape in his capacity as High Commissioner for South Africa.

The Colonial Government adopted and held to a policy of indirect rule through the chiefs, the outcome demonstrating the truth of Mosesh's words to Sir George Grey: "If only you will rule my people through me there will be no trouble. They will follow me, and I will follow you." The British Government's instructions to Sir Marshall Clarke were brief "that nothing more should be attempted at first than the protection of life and property, and the maintenance of order on the border . . . (while) the Basuto were to be encouraged to establish internal self-government sufficient to suppress crime and settle internal tribal disputes." 1 (Lagden op. cit. p. 560).

"This neat coincidence of interest between private altruism and government parsimony set a pattern of administration which was to last, in varying degrees and despite attempts at improvement, into the fourth and fifth decades of the next century!" 2 (Spence op. cit. p. 222)

The initial advantages of British administration, which had adapted itself to the existing social and economic organisation of Basuto social structure were lost with the inevitable development and emergence of new social, political and economic problems. The great increase in the population combined with an unchanged traditional agricultural system and the dangerous increase of soil erosion created a situation where the Basuto men were forced to sell their labour in South Africa in order to survive. Allied to this were factors related to chieftainship and land tenure, all hindering the development which otherwise might have taken place. On the 3rd March 1910 a proclamation providing for the establishment of the Basutoland Council "for discussing the domestic affairs of the territory" was made. It consisted of a president, (the Resident Commissioner) and not more than a hundred members. The Paramount Chief was to be a member under the title of Chief Councillor and had the right to nominate ninety-four persons belonging to the Basuto tribe who were to include "the principal persons exercising authority as chiefs of the Basuto tribe". If the Resident Commissioner confirmed the nominees, they were then appointed by him. In addition the Resident Commissioner appointed five members. The powers of the council were those of advice and criticism. This council, though a step forward, in no way took the place of the traditional Pitso, developed by Moshesh, a gathering of all the people where more or less all were free to express opinions and voice grievances.

The great drought of 1932-3 and the crushing effects of worldwide depression exposed the gravity of Basutoland's problems. It was during this time that the famous old type Basuto pony almost disappeared. When the rains did come they were torrential, making the erosion worse. The situation was grave, and a commission was sent out, under Sir Adam Pim. The Pim Report recommended immediate reform in the structure of administration and a grant of £151 000 over ten years to deal with the more urgent soil erosion problems. Chief Griffith, who had been Paramount Chief for thirty years, associated himself with these reforms. Chief Griffith died in 1939 and was succeeded by the young progressively minded Chief Seeiso, who also commenced a programme of reform. It was a serious blow when Seeiso died in 1940, leaving an infant son and his chief widow, Mantsebo, as Regent. She was challenged by Seeiso's halfbrother, Bereng, but defeated his claims in the courts. Bereng, despite being a Catholic, resorted to using protective medicines to advance his ambitions. These medicines required portions of human flesh and in 1949 Bereng was executed for complicity in murder.

A number of institutional innovations were introduced during these years, amongst which were also: (1) the alteration of authority and composition of the Basutoland Council, (2) the establishment of District Councils, (3) the appointment of a body of Advisers to the Paramount Chief, and (4) the formation of an independent finance committee for regulating the conduct of the national treasury.

In 1946 a National Treasury was finally established, a major development, introduced by the Resident Commissioner, Charles Arden Clarke. In general, the reforms introduced over the period 1938-55 brought about a closer integration of Basuto tribal organisation and the administrative machine. Nevertheless, it seems that forces in Basuto Society seeking genuine reform were much stronger than was realised by the administration of the time. Negotiations for a national constitution took place between 1955 and 1959, and in 1960 the country's first proper written Constitution became operational.

A principal feature of the Constitution was the establishment of a legislative Council, to be known as the Basutoland National Council, consisting of eighty members. Of this number, forty were to be elected from the membership of the nine District Councils. The remaining forty members included four ex-officio Government officers, twenty-two principal or ward chiefs, and fourteen persons selected by the Paramount Chief. The Resident Commissioner, H.E. Mr. A. G. T. Chaplin, was appointed President of the Council for the first year of its existence. A college of chiefs, consisting of all principal and ward chiefs, under the leadership of the Paramount Chief was given the duties of recognising chiefs, investigating complaints against chiefs and adjudicating disputes over succession and boundaries.

Prince Bereng Seeiso, son of the Paramount Chief Seeiso's second wife, Mabereng, and one of the best educated of his generation, returned from Oxford in 1959 and assumed the Paramountcy. Characterising the paramountcy in Basutoland, even today, is a certain tension in Moshesh's own legendary clan, the Bakuena, in which the 'Sons of Moshesh' have always been in direct control and to which all but three of the major chiefs belong. (Bakuena meaning 'people of the crocodile', from the time of the famous old chief Kuena, the crocodile. Hence the crocodile as the national emblem, even though this creature is completely unknown in Lesotho.) A certain amount of resentment was felt by subordinate chiefs and many of them resisted the encroaching power of the paramountcy. Although self-rule was considered desirable by the chiefs, they also had reasonable fears that this kind of political advancement would curtail their own powers without adequate compensation.

The general election of January 1960, following the promulgation of the 1959 Constitution was the first election based on modern British electoral practice to be held in Basutoland. Competing for ascendency were firstly, the Basutoland Congress Party under the leadership of Ntsu Mokhehle (M.Sc. Fort Hare) and a Pan Africanist. Although not basically a communist orientated party, it has several avowed communists among its members. The Congress Party, carrying the colours red, black and green, campaigned rigorously demanding immediate independence, rapid Africanisation of the civil service, and the withdrawal of the Church from politics. The other major political party at the time was the Basutoland National Party, founded in 1958 by Leabua Jonathan and G. C. Manyeli – both prominent Catholics. The B.N.P. had as one of its chief aims, the resoration of 'the ancient democratic relationship of the chiefs and the people'. (Dundas & Ashton, op. cit. p. 52.) In its manifesto it also proclaimed the party's dependence upon God, its support for hereditary chieftainship and loyalty to the British Crown. Although Catholic missionaries were inclined to support the B.N.P., actual political involvement was minimal. The third party competing was the Marema-Tlou Freedom Party, made up of a merger between the Marema-Tlou party, founded in 1957 by Chief S. S. Matete and the Basutoland Freedom Party led by B. M. Khaketla, formerly Deputy-President of the Congress Party from which he broke way in 1960. The new Marema-Tlou Freedom Party was headed by Chief Matete as President and Khaketla, known as one of the 'new' intellectuals and a powerful writer in both Sesuto and English, as Vice-President. The Party declared its policy as the attainment of economic self-sufficiency, the revision of the whole approach to agriculture and land tenure, commerce and education. After unsuccessful appeals for aid in Western Europe and the United States, support was sought from various African States and possibly too, from the Soviet Union. (Stevens, Lesotho, Botswana and Swaziland, op. cit. p. 64.) The election results gave a dominating position to the B.C.P. with thirty-six percent of the popular vote. The Marema-Tlou Freedom Party polled only 8 percent of the votes. With a new government established, Basutoland became the first of the High Commission Territories, (Botswana and Swaziland being the other two), to be brought into the stream of African Constitutional evolution.

The next five years saw the establishment of a Constitutional Commission which toured the whole country receiving testimony on important points, amongst which were the status of the Paramount Chief, the status of Basutoland, the relationship between Britain and Basutoland, franchise, function of the chiefs and the future of the Basuto courts.

With South Africa no longer a member of the Commonwealth, relationships became somewhat complicated. Adding to the complication was the growing number of South African political refugees escaping to Basutoland. This was an embarrassment to British authorities, and even the B.C.P. saw the danger of these extremists becoming involved in Basutoland politics. South Africa imposed severe border restrictions, and independence for Basutoland became a realistic objective from both British and Basuto points of view.

The Constitutional Commission completed its work and its recommendations were released in October 1963. Amongst these were: (1) rapid transition to independence in 1965;

with separate citizenship and flag under the name Lesotho; (2) establishment of a constitutional monarchy under Moshoeshoe II, the Paramount Chief Bereng Seeiso; (3) establishment of a National Assembly consisting of an upper and lower house of elected members; (4) a cabinet on the British model; and (5) Universal franchise. Formerly there had been only male suffrage.

After prolonged negotiations between the existing government and British authorities an agreement in principle was reached. A feature of the negotiations had been B.C.P. antipathy and distrust of the Republic of South Africa. But once independence had been assured, and the various political parties revived their efforts for support of the electorate, basic economic realities began to shift influence away from the B.C.P. In 1963, 52 000 Basutos were employed in the South African goldmining industries; earning approximately R8 000 000, of which R775 310 was sent directly to families in Basutoland. There was a general tendency toward ideas of promoting peace, support of South African law and opposition of Communism. Despite danger signals the dominant B.C.P. maintained its strong ideological attachment to Pan-Africanism.

Chief Jonathan, at the head of the B.N.P., came out forcefully for the strongest possible economic ties with the Republic. Although opposing South Africa's racial policies, which he said could not last indefinitely, he expressed a firm hope that Basutoland might become the first Black African state to establish diplomatic relations with the Republic. The B.N.P.'s strong denunciation of Communism won it the support of the Church and the South African Government.

The Marema-Tlou Freedom Party had once again split into two factions; the M.F.P. being led now by Dr. Seth Mokotoko and Chief Matete reviving the Marema-Tlou Party. Each party was identified with a symbol, and Government Information teams covered the whole country explaining the identification symbols for the elections; (B.N.P., a cow; B.C.P. a knobkierrie; Marema-Tlou, an elephant; M.F.P. an open hand) and also general election procedures. The B.N.P. won the election by a narrow majority, gaining 31 of the 60 seats in the National Assembly; the B.C.P. took 25 seats and M.F.P. with 4 seats.

In a past election speech, Chief Jonathan reaffirmed his desire to initiate conversations with the Prime Minister of South Africa, Dr. Verwoerd, and announced that so long as he was directing the affairs of his country he would not allow into Maseru a single embassy of any Communist country or of countries with Communist sympathies including Ghana, Tanzania and the Arab countries. The day following the elections, Sir Alexander Giles relinquished his post as the last Resident Commissioner of Basutoland and Moshoeshoe II was sworn in as Her Majesty's Representative. Ironically, Chief Jonathan had not been elected in his own constituency and a by-election, brought about by the resignation of John M. Mothepu, B.N.P. member in a 'safe' mountain constituency was held. As member of the Assembly and head of the B.N.P. he then became Lesotho's first Prime Minister.

ECONOMY

This mini-state Lesotho, operates on a budget smaller than that of most larger advertising agencies. The average per capita income is R60,00 per annum. An analysis of the economic structure is tragically simple. This is an agricultural country in which the yearly agricultural output has been pitifully inadequate, becoming more so each year with a growing population.

AGRICULTURE

One third of the country is arable, the other two thirds are virtually impenetrable mountains. Grazing in the mountains is really only suitable for sheep and goats. The reasons for the general failure of agriculture in Lesotho can be summed up under the following headings.

(1) LAND TENURE. All land in Lesotho is owned by the Nation. In the days of Moshesh I, he was, in fact, responsible for all land grazed and tilled by the people owing allegiance to him. Today, land in Lesotho is the responsibility of the Chieftainship headed by the Paramount Chief, now the King of Lesotho. Ownership of the land can never be allocated, only the right to use it. There are two kinds of land-use. Semi-permanent rights are granted for schools, churches, administration buildings, housing, hospitals, trading stores, gardens, playgrounds and now, with negotiation, industrial sites. Since 1961 semi-permanent rights were granted for diamond-mining to Basuto only. The temporary or seasonal rights are given to the Basuto as individuals only for the express purpose of growing traditional crops. That this system of land allocation is an impediment to progressive agriculture is obvious, particularly when viewed in conjunction with the second consideration.

(2) COMMUNAL CUSTOMS AND TRADITIONS. The seasonal allocation of land for traditional crops, means just that. And the traditional crops are maize, wheat and sorghum. These are one-season crops and fit into the concept of communal grazing of the land. After a man has harvested his crop, his community has the right to feed its stock on the remains. So the planting of a cash-crop would interfere with communal rights. For example, potatoes would be planted in the later winter, just when the cattle come down from the mountains to avoid the extreme cold and feed on the remains of the sorghum harvests. Livestock owners would object to such a cash crop. Custom and tradition is also opposed to fences, as they interfere with communcal grazing rights and footpaths. Proper fencing would not only contribute to better management and control of arable land and grazing, but would also release approximately 66 000 herdboys whose occupation deprives them of education and training in industrial skills. (*Stevens op. cit. p. 109).

(3) Agriculture in Lesotho has traditionally been the concern of the women of the community. Originally land was tilled by the women with hoes. Contact with Europeans in the

middle of the nineteenth century saw the introduction of the plough, which encouraged men to a little more involvement in agriculture.

(4) But with the discovery of diamonds and gold in the Republic, the phenomenon of migrant labour came about, becoming an increasingly dominant factor in the economy. It drew men away from the land, but today still provides a steady income as well, which is not affected by crop disease, erosion and droughts.

(5) Backward farming practice such as overgrazing, erosion, lack of irrigation and soil conservation, combined to impoverish the little arable land available. Even with money available, cattle are wealth. A young man traditionally pays his bride's father 15 cows before the marriage. The country is far more suited to sheep and goats, which seem to be able to provide an exceptionally high quality wool and mohair in the cool mountainous regions. However, the lack of selective breeding lowers the quality of both wool and mohair. Also, even inferior cattle are considered a better investment than goats.

(6) The final point to consider now is the British policy of minimal government. Because of the rather strange nature of the colonisation, that is, colonisation by request for protective reasons, Britain followed a policy of non-interference with local traditions and practises. This had the resulting disadvantage that Britain did not feel directly responsible for any intensive development schemes until the early fifties, when the gravity of the situation could no longer be ignored.

To sum up: the country has a comparatively low agricultural yield and carrying capacity which could be vastly improved with an intensification of land reforms, education and progressive farming programmes. At the moment wool, mohair and hides are the most significant products, with wool exports in 1970 totalling 10 438 580 lbs. and mohair 2 162 619 lbs.

Wheat exports: 150 000, 200 lb. bags in 1969. While in 1970 347 940, 200 lb. bags of maize had to be imported, maize being the staple food of the Basuto.

In 1967 the Central Planning and Development Office published a five-year development plan. In this plan top priority is given to the development of agriculture. Out of the 28,8 million rand worth of development expediture over the five-year period, 6,5 million rand will be directed toward agricultural and live-stock development. Effort is to be channelled into greater use of fertilizer, crop research, mechanisation, irrigation, soil and water conservation, with special emphasis, too, being given to livestock production. Projects will include quality improvement of woolproducing sheep, mohair goats, cattle and poultry farming.

A soil survey has been carried out by the Lesotho National Development Corporation, in preparation for the production of cherries and asparagus for export. This project is to be established in the northern districts of Leribe, in collaboration with a United Nations development programme, and will link up with proposed food processing factories.

MINERALS

After extensive prospecting, it appears that only diamonds are present in a quantity great enough to merit mining. The Rio Tinto mining company has been involved in a three year exploratory operation at Letsent le Terai, the richest diamond field discovered to date. It has, however, been decided by Rio Tinto that while diamonds are definitely present, they do not justify a large scale mining operation. This does not, however, mean that diamonds will cease to be one of Lesotho's most profitable exports. The nature of the deposits and the terrain in which they are situated make it a pick and shovel proposition, and as such, an extremely interesting one. Diamonds to the value of R651 843,75c were exported in 1970.

LESOTHO'S 'WHITE GOLD': WATER

The country possesses the most important watershed in Southern Africa. The tested physical and chemical purity of the water of the Orange and its tributaries make it especially suitable for domestic and industrial purposes. The Shand Report on the water resources of Lesotho proposes three chemes: (1) The Ox-Bow Scheme, (2) The Kau River Scheme, and (3) The Semena River Scheme. The Ox-Bow scheme could be developed in five stages to supply water and electricity to Lesotho and the Orange Free State. With these five stages complete, the Shand Report estimates that over 350 million kilowatt-hours of energy could be generated per annum, and a steady flow of pure water of 100 million gallons per day delivered at rates highly competitive with those ruling in the areas of supply at present. With the constantly increasing demands on the Vaal, Lesotho's water could become indispensable to South Africa's economic development. Apart from the absolute necessity of water and electricity to industrialisation, the secondary benefits of such a scheme, namely irrigation of land otherwise condemned to dry farming methods, and the tremendous tourist attraction of these lakes in the Malutis, would be of vital importance to the economy of Lesotho.

(All figures quoted have been obtained from the Annual Statistical Bulletin for 1970, compiled and issued by the Bureau of Statistics, Maseru.)

INDUSTRY

At the attainment of independence, Lesotho had one of the most discouraging industrial situations in Africa with not a single industry. In 1967, the Prime Minister asked Parliament to form the Lesotho National Development Corporation, a state owned organisation charged with the duty of encouraging investment in the country. This organisation was to present a business appreciation of the investment and expansion opportunities an independent country was able to offer.

Dr. Anton Rupert, honorary Industrial Adviser to Lesotho, was approached and a leading executive from 'Rupert International', Wynand van Graan, a South African with remarkable business instinct, experience and drive, was seconded to Lesotho to become the Managing Director of the Lesotho National Development Corporation. L.N.D.C. started operations with the slogan 'It is better to light one small candle than to curse the darkness'. Appropriately, that was the first light industry launched. A factory producing household candles for export. This was a start. Today it has an export market won entirely on the merits of quality and price.

The guiding principle of the L.N.D.C. is simple. Lesotho would not compete on charity and compromise. It would compete on quality and the principle of expansion generating its own growth. Now, four years later, the breakthrough in Lesotho's development has been achieved. Industrial and other activity has been introduced in areas where there was none. Training is being brought to unskilled people to the extent that the products and the services they render are earning approval in the international market place.

The Corporation's policy is the establishment of economically viable projects to help alleviate the problem of unemployment. Foreign investors are being attracted by the genuine business advantages offered, and for the first time in Lesotho's history business talks and negotiations are being conducted on equal terms. The Corporation has become self-sufficient through its own investments and commercial activities, and more and more companies are being formed. Because of its considerable natural attractions, Lesotho gives first priority to tourism, and the largest L.N.D.C. venture and investment was the establishment of the 'Holiday Inn'. This venture has been remarkably successful, major extensions are taking place, making it one of the largest hotels in Southern Africa. This success has introduced tourism as a stable industry in Lesotho.

Recognised European experts are being brought into the country to introduce in the various ventures the highest possible level of efficiency, quality and trading.

The Royal Lesotho Tapestry Weavers are in full production, producing finest quality handwoven tapestries from mohair. They were awarded a Gold Medal for quality at the 34th International Exhibition of Arts and Crafts in Florence, Italy, in 1970.

The Kolonyama Pottery, in which L.N.D.C. is one of the directors, has become known for the outstanding quality of its products, and much of the work is already being performed by Basutos being trained at the pottery.

A highly qualified German goldsmith has started the 'Royal Crown' Goldsmithing works, training Basuto goldsmiths and producing exquisite and sophisticated jewellery.

The Corporation is aiming at the development of Lesotho into one of Southern Africa's leading handicraft centres, and is at present negotiating further projects for an Italian Shoe workshop and the making of leather handbags.

In the purely industrial field L.N.D.C. has established itself, or been instrumental in establishing, a variety of other concerns. The Maphutsoa area, opposite Ficksburg is being developed as another industrial site, with an electric lamp and lightfitting factory, already in production. This project is being managed by an Italian concern, owning one of the largest factories of this kind in Florence. The factory has its own brass foundry and has started casting superb quality belt and shoe buckles as a subsidiary product. Included in the Ficksburg bridge industrial complex is a clothing factory and a fertilizer blending and packing plant. The foundation of food processing factories is being researched.

Another interesting venture is the diamond cutting and polishing works in Maseru. Negotiations were successfully concluded with Israeli concerns, and the Lesotho Diamond Works came into operation in March 1971. This is one of the only diamond cutting works employing and training Africans. At present the company is supplied with diamonds by approximately a thousand diggers in the mountains. This is precision work, involving an overall training period of five years. As an indication of how significant this project could become for Lesotho, consider that in Israel, diamond cutting works employ over ten thousand workers and in 1970 exported polished stones to the value of 250 million dollars. Already the Lesotho Diamond Works are handling stones worth a hundred thousand rand every month.

A major achievement by the Government's Central Planning and Development Office was the publication in 1971 of Lesotho's first five year development plan. In this document the development priorities of Lesotho, Agriculture, Education and the establishment of a Lesotho National Development and Savings Bank are clearly set out. The primary purpose of the Bank will be the mobilization of savings, the promotion of credit in the private sector and the formulation of investment proposals and schemes in agriculture and local industry.

Within this framework of the Government's Five Year Plan, the L.N.D.C.'s activities will increase to an extent where they could substantially change the economic course of events in Lesotho and bring the country much closer to economic self-sufficiency.

COMMUNICATIONS

Commerce and trade in the interior of Lesotho has always been governed by one overriding factor; the almost total absence of roads. Trading stores were built in the mountains by European traders who supplied the Basuto with consumer goods in return for wool, mohair, maize, wheat, sorghum and hides. All building materials and trading stocks were transported by donkeys along bridlepaths. This network of paths traverse the country as organically as the blood vessels of the human body supply the tissues with blood. How the bridlepaths, zig-zagging up and down almost impossible inclines, and along treacherous precipices, were constructed by untrained communal labour is an engineering riddle. The Mountain Road, the only properly constructed road penetrating the Malutis, was built in 1955 and the engineers used the existing bridlepaths almost exclusively for plotting the course of this road across range upon range of precipitous mountains.

In 1942, Frasers Ltd., one of the original trading concerns in Lesotho, purchased 500 donkeys from farmers in the South African Karoo, for use in transporting building materials into the mountains. So gruelling was the going and the climate that not a single donkey survived the first Maluti winter.

The cost of road-building in these mountains is extremely high and so the most obvious alternative is air-travel. The first flight into the mountains was a headline-making mercy flight by the South African Air Force during World War II. After several attempts the air-craft landed at Makhotlong, to take a seriously ill woman to hospital in Pietermaritzburg. Subsequently some small South African based companies organised scheduled and non-scheduled operations between Mokhotlong, Semongkong, Tlokoeng and Maseru. These did not run with regularity and by 1952 had almost ceased. In the mid-forties, Dick Southworth, flight instructor in the South African Air Force, began exploratory flights into the territory. Using an instinct and skill which have since become legendary, he was able to land his single-engined plane at the most isolated posts and supervise the laying-out of landing strips. From this, Lesotho's first air-charter service, 'Basutair' came into existence, with a small fleet of air-craft and piloted by men trained rigorously by Mr. Southworth in the art of flying and landing under extremely variable and dangerous conditions.

By 1969 there were thirty-two landing strips and in January 1969, 1 200 flights originated from Maseru. In 1968, the Lesotho Government in conjunction with 'Basutair' and in a pool agreement with South African Airways introduced a twice weekly Dakota Service, between Maseru and Johannesburg. In December 1969, 'Basutair' was officially taken over by the Lesotho Government and was established by L.N.D.C. as Lesotho's state airline, called Lesotho Airways Corporation, handling all internal air traffic and regular flights between Maseru and Johannesburg. The Maseru/Johannesburg run has been improved by the introduction of a South African Airways Hawker-Siddeley 748 aircraft, increasing the service from two to three flights per week.

ROADS

European grants have made possible the construction of a tarred highway linking the major towns in the foothills and extending north/south for approximately 250 kilometres. Subsidiary roads to missions and places of interest in the foothills are usually quite adequate for sight-seeing trips, and wind through superbly picturesque scenery.

THE CHURCH

Significantly, the first missionaries came to Lesotho at the specific wish of Moshesh I. Having heard of the White man's religion and certain Christian principles, Moshesh became convinced that this teaching would be of great value to the Basuto. He communicated his wishes to Adam Krotz, a Griqua leader living at Philippolis, accompanying his message with a handsome gift of cattle. The three young French missionaries of the ''Société des Missions Évangéliques in Paris,'' fired with missionary zeal had set out in search of a people to whom they could bring their doctrine. Incredible but true, fate brought them to Adam Krotz, who immediately told them of the Mountain King, Moshesh, and his desire to have his people taught the principles of Christianity. Three weeks later, on the 28th of June 1833, Casalis, Arbouset and Gosselin arrived at Thabu Bosiu, where they were warmly welcomed by Moshesh. In no time at all they had trained Basuto teacher-evangelists, who conducted small churches and schools over a wide area, sitting down among the people as their French instructors had sat down at Morija, Mission headquarters; creating around them a Christian Community in which the aim was 'participation'. The Church belonged to the Basuto people, as it has continued to belong ever since. This was made particularly real by the fact that the French mission had no hierarchy. Church matters were settled in committee and once a Basuto became a Christian he found he had a voice in Christian affairs. The missionaries brought their wives with them and made Lesotho their home. Their children, born in Lesotho, grew up speaking Sesotho from childhood, continuing to do their fathers work, sharing in the life around them.

In 1862 the first two Roman Catholic priests came to Lesotho and were, as had been the French missionaries, welcomed by Moshesh. They were Bishop Jean-Francais Allard and Father Joseph Gerard, both of the congregation of the Oblates of Mary Immaculate, a group formed in Provence by Eugene de Mazenod, which had received its name and papal approval in 1826. Moshesh observed to those who questioned his decision in welcoming the Catholics, that churches were like doctors; it was best to consult more than one! The Catholics were given Tloutle, a sheltered valley about 40 kilometres from Maseru, and under the guidance of Father Gerard the settlement Roma developed, today the largest Roman Catholic centre in Southern Africa.

In 1876 the Anglican Church established its first missions at Leribe and Mohale's Hoek, from which, always with severe financial difficulties, they gradually extended. There is today a small Anglican pro-cathedral in Maseru and the Church runs some of the best schools in the country. There are other denominations represented in Lesotho, making valuable contributions in the fields of medicine and education. The chief protagonists are the French Protestants and the Roman Catholics – two churches profoundly different in character.

The Churches have for a considerable time played an extremely important role in the life of Lesotho. Ninety per cent of the country's education is in their hands; they run hospitals, train priests, teachers and nurses, operate printing presses and publish newspapers, and exercise a profound influence on the social life of the Basuto. They are also the chief patrons of music and literature; a great deal of Lesotho's intellectual life owes its origins to the Churches.

After the first world war, the Catholic Oblates appealed for assistance to their congregation in Canada. In 1924 the first Canadian Fathers arrived and the Catholic Church moved into a period of rapid expansion. In 1930 the Vicariate was transferred to the Eastern Province of Canada resulting in the Catholic mission today being mainly a Mosotho and French Canadian one. In 1945 the Canadian Oblates at Roma founded the Pius XII College which developed dramatically into the foremost educational institution in the country. On the 1st of January, 1964, the Pius XII College became the non-denominational University of Lesotho, Botswana and Swaziland. A census in 1956 gave a return of 33 percent Catholics, 21 percent French Protestants, 9 percent Anglicans and 5 percent other Christians. These statistics have remained more or less unchanged.

TOURISM

The gaunt magnificence of the country makes every drive into it a particularly rewarding experience. Most of the roads are unsurfaced, but well constructed and maintained and easily negotiated by the average vehicle. The Mountain Road which runs for a hundred and fifty kilometres into the heart of the Malutis makes a tremendous day's outing from Maseru. In summer there are a dozen places to swim in clear, effervescent mountain streams. In winter the snow and winter colours make it one of the most impressive drives in the world. Another similar but slightly shorter drive is to Malealea. The first half of this drive is along the new tarred road to Mafeteng. Upon reaching the neck, at the point before starting the decline into the Malealea valley, a plaque was mounted earlier this century, bearing the following admonition: 'Warfarer, pause awhile and gaze upon paradise.' No idle boast, and this road is in very good repair.

In the same category is the drive to Pitseng, just beyond Leribe. Three quarters of this drive is on the tarred north-south road, and in autumn, when the cosmos are in bloom it is unforgetable. This trip takes one through Teyateyaneng and its Blue Mountain Inn with its superb view, lovely gardens and good accommodation. While in Teyateyaneng it is well worth visiting 'Tullycraft', an independent carpet-making centre, producing exquisite handknotted mohair rugs of finest quality, created under completely authentic conditions.

A few miles from here, right on the road is the Kolonyama Pottery, built out of converted grain-silos, producing beautiful and original pottery. At Leribe itself is a well known hostelry, Mountain View Hotel, where a midday break can be made.

'Oxfam' have made available a number of excellent 'guides' to the districts. They are written and compiled by David P. Ambrose of the University of Botswana, Lesotho and Swaziland at Roma. They provide detailed maps and descriptions of all the districts, designed to in-form and help the traveller, and also to raise money for the Oxford Committee for Famine Relief.

The 'Oxfam Guide' to the Mokhotlong district includes a detailed map of the 'Roof of Africa Rally' route from Butha Buthe to the Sani Pass. This route presents a challenge for the more adventurous but should not be undertaken without a suitable vehicle (jeep or buggy type) or in poor weather. The Moteng Pass between Butha Buthe and Oxbow takes a lot of nerve but is well worth the strain.

The 'Roof of Africa Rally' is one of the toughest of its kind, lasting two days and running along one of the highest accessible mountain roads in Africa to the Sani Pass in the Drakensberge. In 1971 there were 123 entries. The Rally takes place annually in September.

A very significant tourist development is being planned for these north-eastern mountains of Lesotho in conjunction with the Lesotho National Development Corporation. This is one of the only five places on the African Continent where it is possible to ski. Not far from this area, 3 000 metres high, the giant Malibamatso water scheme is to be developed. The belt around the proposed lake will be proclaimed a National Park with a modern hotel and one or more Swiss style health clinics. The water scheme will include a modern road into the area which will provide for comfortable access.

In the south there are good inns at Mohales Hoek and Quthing and several historically interesting sites to visit. Near Mohales Hoek there are authentic cannibal caves and at Masitise, just off the road between Mohales Hoek and Quthing, is the cave house built and inhabited in 1860 by the distinguished French Protestant missionary, Frederic Ellenberger and his family, which, today, is preserved as a museum.

More accessible to Maseru visitors is Morija. Morija is the original seat of Christianity in Basutoland and has a small but interesting museum, where visitors can view 80 million years old dinosaur footprints, in comfort! There are several places where, by a freak of nature, prehistoric imprints have been preserved, but these are often hard to find and a knowledgeable guide is needed. Some of the more outstanding examples have been reproduced and are kept at the museum.

For those wishing to see more of Lesotho than can be reached by road, the Lesotho Airways Corporation has regular services all over the mountains, which in winter are a world of snow, and in summer provide some of the finest trout streams in Africa. For those in search of an open-air holiday, trekking into the mountains on horse-back, staying in well-equipped rondavels situated near the best fishing areas, as at Semongkong and the Malutsanyane Falls, there is an efficient travel service in Maseru, Maluti Treks. This is in touch too with leading South African travel agencies.

The 'Holiday Inn' Casino in Maseru has become a cosmopolitan meeting place, particularly for those fascinated by the whirring of roulette wheels and ringing of slot machines.

Apart from providing the best accommodation and tourist facilities to visitors, the hotel is elaborately equipped for conferences, and it is the aim of the L.N.D.C. to utilise Lesotho's central location to develop the country into an international conference centre.

A second large tourist complex with a large hotel, horse riding and trout fishing facilities in particular is being planned on the Qeme plateaux not far out of Maseru.

The climate in Lesotho is perfect, bracing and healthy. As mentioned before, health clinics are soon to be featured as one of the country's attractions. The summers are warm, but with refreshingly cool nights. Although this is a summer rainfall area, the rain is in the form of periodic thunderstorms, spectacular and soon over. The winters are particularly stimulating, very dry, brisk and frosty, with brilliant sunshine.

HEALTH SERVICES

These have always been inadequate. Just how inadequate is demonstrated in the following figures: Lesotho has an average of 1 doctor for every 27 000 inhabitants as compared to South Africa's 1 to every 1 800. Small hospitals and clinics are scattered throughout the country, often run by the various missions with larger, better equipped hospitals at Roma, Morija and the Queen Elizabeth II hospital in Maseru. Nearly all patients requiring specialist care have in the past been transferred to hospitals in the Republic of South Africa, the nearest being in Bloemfontein, 150 kilometres away.

Because of the inaccessible nature of the country, most patients with serious illnesses die long before they can be treated. The history of medical services in Lesotho is dominated by several outstanding characters whose lives of absolute dedication both to their profession and the people, stand out like beacons. Unfortunately, it is not within the scope of this text to give an account of these individuals.

An interesting development came about in the late fifties when a private practitioner procured a light aircraft which he used in his practice and which was finally taken by the Oxford Committee for Famine Relief, and became known as the 'Flying Doctor Service'. The plane was used to take the Service's doctor and medical supplies to remote clinics and to bring patients to Maseru for more comprehensive treatment. The Flying Doctor Service is still in operation today.

One of the most interesting recent features of the Lesotho Health Services is the Medical Shuttle Service initiated by Dr. Anton Rupert. This came about when many of South Africa's foremost surgeons and doctors wrote to Dr. Rupert offering their services free of charge as part of the assistance to be given to the Basuto Nation.

In conjunction with the Lesotho Government, Dr. Rupert organised this medical shuttle service between the major cities of the Republic of South Africa and Maseru. Today the scheme is sponsored by the Rupert Organisation as a Community Service.

Every second week a team of leading specialists and theatre staff spend the weekend consulting and operating in the Queen Elizabeth II hospital. Under this Medical Shuttle Service, 290 volunteer specialists have made 114 visits, have performed 1 850 operations and given 4 587 consultations. 300 theatre sisters have accompanied the doctors and not one patient has died under operation. (These figures are as up until July 1972.)

INDEX OF PHOTOGRAPHS

BIBLIOGRAPHY

Becker, P., "Day of Destiny".

Casalis, E., "The Basuto".

Coates, A., "Basutoland".

Ellenberger, D. F. (VDM)

MacGregor, J. C., "History of the Basuto. Ancient and Modern".

Germond, R. C., "Chronicles of Basutoland".

Pollock and Agnew, "An Historical Geography of South Africa".

Rosenthal, Eric, "African Switzerland".

Sheddick, V. (PhD. London), "Land Tenure in Basutoland".

Smith, E., "The Mabilles of Basutoland".

Stevens, R. P., "Lesotho, Botswana and Swaziland".

Stockly, G. M. (A.R.O., D.I.C., A.I.M.M., F.G.S.), "Report on Geology of Basd". utolan

Theal, G. M., "A Fragment of Basuto History".

Tylden, G., "A History of Thaba Bosiu".

Tylden, G., "The Rise of the Basuto".

Tylden, G., "Early days in Maseru".

"Basutoland Year Book". 1962.

"Basutoland. Report for the year, 1963".

"Lesotho". 1967.

"Chairman's Report, Lesotho National Development Corporation". 1971.

"Progress reports, Lesotho National Development Corporation".

PHOTOGRAPHY

Pages 14, 15, 17, 19, 29, 30, 34, 35, 45, 48, 50, 61 – W. van der Kallen

Pages 23, 24, 27, 37, 39, 42, 43, 57 – Bob Morrison

Pages 9, 58, 59 – Andrew Smallwood